Wessex Tales

THOMAS HARDY

Guide written by

Ron Simpson

A *Letts* EXPLORE **Liter**

First published 1997

Letts Educational
Aldine House
Aldine Place
London W12 8AW
0181 740 2266

Text © Ron Simpson 1997

Typeset by Jordan Publishing Design

Text design Jonathan Barnard

Cover and text illustrations Hugh Marshall

Design © BPP (Letts Educational) Ltd

British Library Cataloguing in Publication Data
A CIP record for this book is available from the British Library

ISBN 1 85758 628 X

Printed and bound in Great Britain
by Ashford Colour Press, Gosport, Hampshire

Letts Educational is the trading name of BPP (Letts Educational) Ltd

■ Contents

OUT

0   1   2 miles

LOWER   WESSEX

Who's who: character types

Lovers

Lovers

Five of the seven stories in *Wessex Tales* are predominantly love stories. The sets of lovers vary greatly, as do their situations in life, but they are linked in that their love is always beset by **misfortune** and **misunderstanding**. Lovers fail to understand their own feelings or the loved one's character and intentions, they rush into incorrect factual assumptions or are blighted by stubbornness. The situation is usually made worse by the working of chance or coincidence. In several of the tales you should ask yourself whether Hardy is showing Fate working against them or whether they are in fact responsible for their own sufferings.

Only in 'The Distracted Preacher' is there a happy ending, one which Hardy disclaims in his 1912 note about the tale. In this story, the treatment of love is light-hearted and the constant misunderstandings and self-deception of the preacher are (mainly) amusing. In all the other tales, lovers are doomed to grief and sometimes death by bad luck (Fate?) and their own silliness, indecisiveness or over-boldness. The lovers in 'The Melancholy Hussar' are touching in their youth, goodness and loneliness, but they make all the wrong decisions and coincidence works against them. 'Fellow-Townsmen' offers a series of contrasts in loving relationships (and unloving marriage); the essential sadness of the story lies in the waste caused by Lucy and Barnet's lack of understanding of each other's feelings and their unfailingly bad timing. 'Interlopers at the Knap' is a less sad, even slightly cynical, commentary on a similar situation. Again we are looking at more mature people over a span of years (both Barnet and Darton begin as prosperous men of substance) and in both stories chance plays its part. What are the differences, in the characters themselves and in the reader's reactions, between Lucy's loss of Barnet and Sally's rejection of Darton?

Finally, the oddest love story is 'The Withered Arm'. Rhoda Brook's love turns to jealousy, but she is unable to control her power and a macabre horror story ensues. There is a sympathetic presentation of rejected love, but this slides into a violent tale of death and primitive superstition.

Soldiers

You may think it surprising that, in seven stories set in an apparently peaceful part of rural England, two should be about soldiers. This is due in part to Hardy's fascination with the past and, in particular, with the French Revolutionary War (which ended with the Peace of Amiens in 1802) and the Napoleonic War (which resumed hostilities a year later). Hardy later wrote a verse drama, *The Dynasts*, about the Napoleonic War and it was another Thomas Hardy of Dorset, a relation of the writer, who was captain of HMS *Victory* at Trafalgar.

In the years up to 1805, when the Battle of Trafalgar eased the tension, there was a major invasion scare along the South Coast – the background to 'A Tradition of Eighteen Hundred and Four' and 'The Melancholy Hussar of the German Legion'.

You may also be surprised at the British army containing German regiments. Germany was still divided into many small states and King George III of Britain (and of Hanover) had considerable German possessions. Young Germans, owing loyalty to their monarch, could thus find themselves fighting as part of the British Army: there were, for instance, many German regiments involved in the American War of Independence (1775–83).

Rustics

If you are familiar with any of the novels of Thomas Hardy, you will be familiar with his use of rustic characters: simple, uneducated Wessex country men and women. Often the main characters are of a slightly higher class (they may own a farm or have a better education), but the rustics offer much to the novels. They play the part of the **Chorus** in a Greek tragedy: commenting on characters and action, filling in the narrative and providing a **moral code** against which the main action is set. They may serve as *confidants* to the main characters, listening to their problems and sharing them. More often they are, singly or in groups, the source of much **humour**.

'The Three Strangers' depends totally on such rustic characters for its mystery, humour and irony, but they are to be found in many of the tales. In different ways, the milkers in 'The Withered Arm', Mr Darton's philosophical friend Japheth Johns in 'Interlopers at the Knap' and the chaotic chorus of smugglers and officers in 'The Distracted Preacher' are all typical Hardy rustics. Do you think that Rhoda Brook should be included in this group? Is Hardy's presentation of her different from that of the other rustic characters? It may help you to look at differences in speech between her and the others.

The Professions

A large proportion of the characters in Hardy's novels and short stories do work directly connected with the land. The prosperous are often farmers or hay merchants, the poorest labourers or furze cutters, with shepherds, dairymen and so on in between. There are, in a sense, two sorts of "professional" people whose work is specialised. The **conventional professions**, such as school-teacher, doctor, lawyer or vicar, do not usually play a large part in Hardy's fiction, but they are there. In *Wessex Tales*, a preacher is the central figure of a story (and its romantic lead!), but the most unusual set of characters appears in 'Fellow-Townsmen'. Here Hardy places the whole story within the professional classes of a town: the two men are described at the beginning as "fellow-burgesses" so we know we are amongst the urban middle class. The main characters are a man of fortune and his social-climbing wife, a lawyer and his wife, a doctor and an artistic young lady who gets work as a teacher.

The second group of "professionals" are those who have **specialised roles** within country life. They are not educated, but are separated from others by gifts and training and are often people of mysterious power. The hangman is such a figure: hangmen, of course, have an important part to play in two of these tales. Most interesting of all is the "conjuror". He is not a conjuror in our modern sense of the word. How many of the following apply to him instead: magician, wizard, healer, clairvoyant, witch doctor, astrologer? Why do you think that he has such power over the characters in 'The Withered Arm'? The conjuror is a frequent figure in Hardy novels: Conjuror Trendle himself is referred to in *Tess of the D'Urbervilles* and Michael Henchard's visit to Conjuror Fall is a significant event in *The Mayor of Casterbridge*.

■ Themes

Tradition

Tradition

In all his writing, Hardy makes considerable use of tradition. The stories in *Wessex Tales* are often traditional or pretend to be so. Hardy writes mostly about Wessex some 50 or more years before his own time. He claims to know about the events in his stories, which he often treats as factual, by having been told them by aged acquaintances. Therefore many of these stories are presented as being part of an **oral tradition** (passed on by word of mouth). Re-read the opening pages of each of these stories and find how many Hardy sets in the not-too-distant past – typically the early or middle years of the 19th century, the tales being written in about 1880. Then see if Hardy tells us how he obtained the story: does he claim it is local history or a part of the oral tradition, told to him by an aged acquaintance? Interestingly enough, Hardy's own preface tells us that 'The Withered Arm' is based on actual tradition, but that he invented 'A Tradition of Eighteen Hundred and Four', only to find that such a tradition existed.

Hardy also makes great use of **country traditions** within the tales. It is useful to make your own list of these traditions, for example:

● traditions of hospitality in 'The Three Strangers';

● the music in the same story;

● traditional beliefs and superstitions in 'The Withered Arm';

● a village tradition (smuggling) in 'The Distracted Preacher'.

It is worth mentioning that Hardy's tales are soundly based historically as well as using traditions – particularly in the tales of the Revolutionary and Napoleonic Wars, which also deal with events such as King George III establishing Weymouth as a fashionable place to meet.

Wessex

Wessex

Wessex is the setting for these stories and also a major theme. The phrase **Hardy's Wessex** suggests more than just a place: it implies a set of characters and attitudes, almost becoming a character itself. Hardy's reputation as one of the great writers of regional fiction is secure: despite his name-changes, the spirit of the West Country fills his novels and stories. On pages 4–5 there is a map of Wessex, showing all the places mentioned in the *Tales*. In most cases we can easily identify the real town or village behind Hardy's fictitious name.

Wessex was the name of the most powerful of the Saxon kingdoms, ruled in the ninth century by King Alfred the Great. Choosing this name shows Hardy's pride in his native region and its traditions. All the *Wessex Tales* (and most of his novels) are set in what he called South Wessex – really Dorset, where Hardy was born, lived most of his life and died. Hardy's Wessex extends beyond Dorset: its borders go west into Somerset and north as far as Oxford (Christminster in *Jude the Obscure*), but its heart is Dorset and, especially, Dorchester (Casterbridge). Budmouth (Weymouth), Sherton Abbas (Sherborne) and Port Bredy (Bridport) are among other towns which appear in *Wessex Tales* and throughout Hardy's fiction. Egdon Heath, a combination of various heaths near Dorchester, is another key element in Hardy's Wessex: ancient, forbidding, mysterious and full of tradition.

You should make use of a map of Wessex in any study of Hardy's fiction: the paths of characters in different tales or different novels often cross and meet within the same ancient ways.

Chance

Chance

Chance plays a large part in Hardy's fiction. Some critics feel that his use of coincidence can be excessive and unconvincing. However, it is part of a general gloomy (but oddly heroic) world view in which humans are faced with a malevolent **Fate** that steadily destroys them. Hardy's last two novels, written shortly after *Wessex Tales* was published, were attacked for their un-Christian view of the world:

11

instead of God looking after the characters, Fate destroys them. The ending of *Tess of the D'Urbervilles* describes "the President of the Immortals" finishing his "sport" with Tess while *Jude the Obscure* tells the story of an increasingly hopeless battle against Fate.

Wessex Tales does not feature the same, oppressive Fate, but there is widespread use of chance and coincidence. 'The Three Strangers' finds mystery and amusement in coincidence, but more freqently chance leads the characters to make mistakes that destroy their happiness. Quite often, chance conceals information from the characters until it is too late to do them good. You should be able to find many examples of Hardy's use of chance and coincidence; you can then decide for yourself whether you think it makes the stories more or less convincing.

Mystery

Mystery

There is much mystery to enjoy in Hardy's *Wessex Tales*, and it takes many different forms. Mystery of the problem-solving, **"whodunnit"** variety appears in 'The Three Strangers' and the earlier stages of 'The Distracted Preacher'. In the latter, much of the fun derives from the fact that the "detective" (Mr Stockdale) is much slower to elicit the truth than we are as readers. Later, of course, the interest switches to how he will act on his knowledge, but first we are treated to the hunt for the tubs with Latimer – another incompetent detective. Mystery also lies beneath much of 'Fellow-Townsmen': what did various characters really do at key stages in the story?

The most effective use of mystery comes in the creation of a world which is not completely clear-cut and logical, a world in which strangers appear from the night, relations re-appear without warning and Conjuror Trendle has "powers other folks have not". This form of mystery ties in with the use of **superstition**: see what examples you can find of superstitious belief.

Humour

Humour

There is much that is gloomy or tragic in Hardy's fiction, but it is not without its humour. Some is derived from the dialogue of the rustics, for example, in much of 'The Three Strangers' or from such characters as Japheth Johns, the milkers or Solomon Selby, the narrator of 'A Tradition of Eighteen Hundred and Four'. Hardy is quite capable of inserting such humour in a story that is for the most part sad or even tragic. There is also the occasional humorous **set-piece**, notably the hunt for the tubs.

However, a little humour is also derived from Hardy's attitude to his central characters. Does he empathise with them in their problems and sufferings, or does he observe them, kindly enough, from a distance without sharing their emotions? In the latter case he can treat them humorously. In which of the *Wessex Tales* do you think that this treatment applies?

Essays

In the section **Coursework essays**, five possible themes for your coursework assignments are analysed. As you are likely to be using *Wessex Tales* for a Wide Reading assignment, each of these compares Hardy's stories with a 20th-century author (or authors). In the main Text commentary, this icon marks material that will be of particular use for these coursework assignments. In each case the essay subject involved is identified and a relevant quotation or piece of advice is given.

■ Text commentary

Thomas Hardy and the *Wessex Tales*

Thomas Hardy (**1840–1928**) was born in Higher Bockhampton, a village near Dorchester, and at first was articled (employed as a professional apprentice) to an architect and church restorer. His early literary ambitions were to be a poet, but that proved to be his second claim to fame in a remarkable career. Hardy's years as a published novelist ran from 1871 to 1896; after *Jude the Obscure* (1896) he wrote no new full-length novels. The reasons for this were complex, but there is some truth in the theory that he was worn down by constant public criticisms of his work as un-Christian and immoral. Although he had been writing poems all his adult life, his first published collection, *Wessex Poems*, did not appear until 1898. The final thirty years of his life brought fame as a poet (and, to some extent, as a dramatist) as well as the massive 1912 edition of his novels, which by that time were considered more respectable.

Hardy also wrote short stories for much of his career, often for magazine publication. These ranged from the shortest of tales to **novellas** (short novels, often divided into chapters). *Wessex Tales* was the title he gave to his first collection (1888) and he went on to publish three more collections in the years up to 1913. This guide considers the seven stories which make up *Wessex Tales*. Some modern paperback editions consist of the editor's own selection of Hardy stories from the four collections. These all include several of the *Wessex Tales*, usually taking one of them as the title story. This guide can therefore be used with editions under the title *Wessex Tales* (available in the budget-price *Wordsworth Classics*) or named after one of the tales such as 'The Withered Arm' or 'The Distracted Preacher'.

The Three Strangers

The scene is set in some detail at Shepherd Fennel's home, Higher Crowstairs, a very remote house at the junction of two paths. On the night of a violent rainstorm the shepherd and his wife are celebrating the christening of their daughter. One at a time, three strangers seek shelter from the storm and are welcomed into the party. The first has little to say about himself, but the second, warmed by copious draughts of mead (a strong, alcoholic drink made from honey), tells his story in song: he is the hangman, making his way to Casterbridge to hang Timothy Summers, a sheep-stealer. The third stranger appears in the doorway, but flees in horror at the sight of the hangman. Immediately a gun sounds, warning of a prisoner's escape from Casterbridge gaol. Surely it must be the third stranger! However, when he is finally captured, it emerges that the first stranger was the condemned man and the third stranger his brother, on his way to Casterbridge for a last meeting. Timothy Summers is never recaptured.

The setting

Wessex

Hardy sets this story carefully in **time** and **place**. It happened "fifty years ago" in the 1820s (the tale was written in 1883); the final paragraphs remind us that it is a tale of times past and confirm that the first stranger was never recaptured; while the last sentence roots the story in local tradition.

Tradition

But Hardy presents tradition and the past in a more subtle way than mere dates. References early in the story relate the place and the weather to ancient people and events: Nebuchadnezzar (in the biblical Book of Daniel) and Timon (in Shakespeare's *Timon of Athens*) who both cut themselves off from the world; and the famous battles of Senlac (Hastings) and Crécy (in France) from the Middle Ages.

Rustics

Now look through the story and find objects and details that suggest a traditional way of life: for example, you could include the **serpent** – a huge, snake-shaped wind instrument with a sound like a bassoon that was once popular in rural communities.

Regional fiction

Take note of the opening description: "In spite of its loneliness… the spot… was not more than three miles from a country town."

The use of **place** is equally important in this story. The paths are crucial. Although Higher Crowstairs is a remote place, one path leads to the county town, Casterbridge. The shepherd's dwelling is thus the only place of shelter at hand, but in touch with the town. The reader is unaware of which path the second and third strangers are taking and hence of the direction of their journeys. Incidentally, the paths also add to the sense of the past, having been there "a good five hundred years".

The condemned man

In the early 19th century, there were many capital crimes. People were hanged not only for murder but also for lesser crimes such as sheep-stealing. Hardy takes advantage of this to present Timothy Summers as a sympathetic figure. The account given of him by the people at the party emphasises his poverty, and his boldness in taking a sheep "in open daylight". Examine the description of him near the beginning when he approaches the house, and the account of his behaviour when inside. What sort of a person does Hardy present him as? Compare his manner when talking to his hosts with that of

Humour

the hangman later. Obviously he wishes to deceive them, but he does not appear to be a liar. The only lie he tells has an edge of humour to it: he says he is a wheelwright, referring to the wheels in watches and clocks. It is his coolness (in contrast to his brother) that is most striking. He joins in the choruses of the hangman's song (remind yourself of the words of the third verse). During the hunt, he returns for further refreshment and finds himself joined by the hangman. A pleasant conversation ensues, with just one hint, when the hangman first arrives, that Timothy is not completely at ease.

Rustics

As so often in Hardy, the rustics serve as a **Chorus**, suggesting to the reader what to think about events and characters. Here, in the final hunt, they sympathise with the man who turned thief through poverty and who was bold enough to "hob-and-nob" with the hangman. Not surprisingly, they never manage to capture him.

Mystery

Chance

Chance plays a big part in this story, but Hardy is careful to give reasons for everything that happens. The situation of the house, the rain and the welcoming sounds of the party combine to make it likely that strangers would knock at the door. The three men all have good reasons for being on the road: note that there are reasons why the hangman has had to move to Casterbridge. There are also reasons why people don't recognise each other (except the two brothers): if they have lived in the same area, it has been at different times. So we are not troubled by too much strain of coincidence and can enjoy the mystery.

Mystery

There is much of the enjoyment of a "**whodunnit**" here. We are told enough about the first stranger to arouse our suspicions. For instance, his shoes are clearly not his own. See how many more hints you can find that suggest the possibility of prison. Then Hardy teases us with a pair of "red herrings". At first we begin to think we know who the first stranger is (and we are, of course, right), but, when the third stranger appears and disappears, we dismiss the truth as a red herring and make the same mistake as Shepherd Fennel and his friends.

Irony and misunderstanding

"And surely we've zeed him? That little man who looked in at the door by now, and quivered like a leaf when he zeed ye and heard your song!"

Mystery of a different sort presents itself with the **hangman**. To begin with, he poses riddles (for instance, his trade sets a mark not on him, but on his customers), but the mystery about him grows as the rustics learn more about

Professions

him. His profession sets him aside from ordinary men. Note the paragraph just after the third stranger flees when all the guests back off from "the grim gentleman in their midst". Twice he is compared to the devil, first as the Prince of Darkness and then in the Latin quotation which means "a circle of which the devil was the centre". Compare this devilish identity with the hangman's actual behaviour, both at the party and during the pursuit of Timothy's brother. Is the contrast amusing? How does the reader respond to his song, which sounds like a traditional folk song, with the repeated refrain "simple shepherds all", but gradually assumes significance?

The shepherd, the shepherdess and the guests

Rustics

At the beginning, the rustic characters seem to be the subject of the story. Later they provide a background to the action and a source of humour. Some of the humour lies in the picturesque language and vigorous, rhythmic sentences. Hardy's relish for "country" speech can be found in examples like "Late to be traipsing athwart this coomb – hey?", "quivered like a leaf when he zeed you and heard your song" and many others.

Regional fiction

It is too easy (and wrong) to treat the rustics as identical: there is even variety in their speech patterns, notably that of the hangman.

Humour

The other main humorous device is to give a character one slightly exaggerated characteristic (or two paired characteristics) which dictate(s) his or her actions and words. A particularly amusing example comes with the **constable** (not a full-time officer but a volunteer), who is proud of his office, but has no wish to go chasing criminals late at night. He is the "engaged man of fifty" who earlier in the story was always moving anxiously to be with his fiancée, so he is made hesitant by fear and the wish not to leave her. His excuses (based around the need for his staff of office) and delaying tactics combine amusingly with his pride in his authority. This pride is then comically undermined by his verbal confusion at the point of arrest. "Yer money or yer life!" and "in the name of the fath…" suggest highwayman and priest more than constable, while his explanation to the magistrate is a rare mixture of confusion and dignity.

Shepherdess Fennel is another character in whom Hardy creates humour from one main characteristic or linked characteristics. Examine the story to find the humour in her patterns of speech and action.

Hardy's style

It is impossible to generalise about the style in which this story is written. There is no rustic narrator and much of the tale is told in a style typical of a Victorian writer educated in the classics and the Bible. This preserves a certain detachment from the characters. Yet this educated Victorian is also a man of

Wessex

Wessex and delights in the words, as much as the habits, of his native region. Thus the reader is confronted by quotations from folk song and Latin almost side by side. Hardy expects his reader to savour the recipe for the best mead as well as references to medieval history.

Certain elements of Hardy's style are worth emphasising, however. Even his prose writing contains poetic features. In this story, the **imagery** and **detailed observation** are striking. Just before the first stranger's arrival, there is a description of the dance at its height in the sentence beginning, "And so the dance whizzed on…" Note the exhilarating combination of the planet imagery with the down-to-earth observation of "the well kicked clock". Shortly afterwards the stranger's examination of the premises (the bee-hives, the utensils catching water, etc.) is precise in its detail. You will be able to find your own examples of imagery and detailed description.

The tale

Chance

What effect does Hardy wish this tale to have on the reader? It is a story of a strange coincidence, certainly, but that could affect the reader in various ways. What do we feel at the end of the story? Where do our sympathies lie? How deeply are we concerned? The ending leaves part of the mystery unsolved: does it satisfy and please the reader?

A Tradition of Eighteen Hundred and Four

As a young boy in 1804, Solomon Selby is watching the sheep at night, with his Uncle Job, an army sergeant, when he falls asleep. On waking, he discovers that two French officers are there, examining the land and a chart of the Channel. Uncle Job then recognises one of them as Napoleon himself, deciding where to land the French troops in an invasion. The officers return to their ship; the invasion never comes.

The anecdote

This is a "**believe it or not**" story. It seems appropriate that it was written at Christmas 1882 because it is the sort of story that is told to captive audiences at festive gatherings, always vouched for "by my own eyes" or by some trustworthy acquaintance. That is why the narrative arrangement is important.

The modern narrator only appears in three paragraphs; nearly all the tale is in the words of Solomon Selby, the old rustic, who is much more convincing for two reasons. His speech is plain and natural, but the reaction of the listeners is equally persuasive. In the last paragraph, Hardy tells us that, "if anything short of the direct testimony of his own eyes could persuade" the listener of the truth of the story, it would be "Solomon Selby's manner of narrating the adventure." We, as readers, feel that if Thomas Hardy was convinced, maybe we ought to be, too.

Rustics

Tradition and history

This short tale is the most obvious use of **oral tradition** in *Wessex Tales*. It is amusing that Hardy admitted to inventing a traditional story, only to find years later that it was a real tradition (not the same as a true story!). The distancing of the story in time is cleverly done without compromising the essential eye-witness element. The Channel Tunnel debate in 1882 reminds the narrator of Solomon Selby's story. Selby has been dead for at least ten years. The narrator is therefore telling us what he heard from an old man in the 1860s or very early 1870s. Essentially the history is accurate (apart from Napoleon's actual reconnaissance of Lulworth Cove), but is presented through the naive eyes of an uneducated Dorset boy with personal knowledge of the invasion scare of the early 1800s.

Tradition

Regional fiction

"Of all the years of my growing up the ones that bide clearest in my mind were eighteen hundred and three, four and five."

Narrative style

If you examine the different types of English used in this story, you will find ingenious **contrasts**. The first two and the final paragraphs are written in

Rustics

correct, even formal English: "withdrawing the stem of his pipe from the dental notch in which it habitually rested" is a rather over-written substitute for "taking his pipe out of his mouth". You will also have no difficulty in finding examples of rustic speech. For instance, Selby explains that he wasn't "afeard" and Uncle Job suffered "wownds".

Humour

There is plenty of **humour**: in Uncle Job's patriotic outbursts ("O that I had got but my new-flinted firelock, that there man should die!" and its near-repetition); and Selby's muddle with foreign words ("the great Alp mountains", "the Proossians").

Wessex

However, the story would be hard to understand if Selby's Wessex dialect were as broad as that used in conversation in some of the stories, such as the opening of 'The Withered Arm'. Go through the story and see how Hardy balances reasonably correct English with enough details to make the reader accept it as Selby's oral narration: dialect words, for instance, or addressing his listeners directly.

The sergeant and the emperor

Soldiers

What does Uncle Job, a foot sergeant, think about the fact that Napoleon, Emperor of France, still leads his own armies? He is "the Corsican ogre" and Job longs for the chance to kill him, but does one soldier have any respect for the other? The story offers a neat picture of a boy's thoughts about war and soldiers in a frightening, but exciting, time of military upheaval. Uncle Job is a man of massive dignity – "he used to know all about these matters" – and fills young Solomon's head with dreams of battles. Napoleon is a mixture of hero, tyrant and familiar bogeyman ("Boney") to frighten the children.

The Melancholy Hussar of the German Legion

Phyllis Grove lives a very secluded life, five miles from fashionable Weymouth. She becomes engaged to Humphrey Gould, a man of good family and little income, though neither of them is passionate about the relationship. Gould departs to Bath and fails to fulfil his promise to return in a few weeks. Gradually Phyllis, in her loneliness, forms a friendship with a sad and homesick German hussar, Matthaus Tina, stationed on the Downs. They decide to escape to France together, prompted not only by their feelings for each other but by his hatred of the army, her father's intolerance and Humphrey's neglect. On the night of the escape Phyllis sees Humphrey return (with a present and apologies at the ready) and decides that she cannot join Matthaus. From there everything goes wrong: Humphrey's gift is an apology for being already married; Matthaus tries to escape; and he and his friend Christoph are caught and executed. The story ends with the hussars' graves and Phyllis' lifelong grief and devotion.

The story

Although this tale is divided into five chapters, it falls very much into the category of **short story**, not that of novella. There is one simple plot and only two real characters: Phyllis Grove and Matthaus Tina. The others exist mainly to prompt them to action. Dr Grove's bullying and unsociability and Humphrey Gould's more amiable neglect drive Phyllis towards an untypically reckless action and Humphrey's return makes her abandon it. Christoph serves to bring out Matthaus' loyalty which, in turn, leads to both their deaths.

Fiction as history

Tradition

The story is set in 1801, at the very end of the French Revolutionary War. After a brief peace, war was to resume in 1803 as the Napoleonic War (as in the previous story). We are given the precise date on the tombstones at the end. However, Hardy uses many other means to express the sense of history in different ways. Look at the opening of Chapter 1 and see how many numbers referring to dates or years you can find: you should be able to find at least five in the first four paragraphs. The result is that we see the past in various forms:

- the imaginings of the narrator on the Downs;
- the oral tradition of tales told to him;
- the specific secret of Phyllis Grove;
- the hard primary evidence of Court records and gravestones.

Who is the narrator?

The story is being told in the 1880s. Do you think the narrator is Hardy himself? What do we learn of the man? Paragraph 4 gives his approximate year of birth: does it tie in with Hardy's? The narrator is clearly a Wessex man who is at home on the Downs, a man who likes hearing the "characteristic

Wessex

tales" of Wessex. He knew Phyllis well and wishes to put her case to save her from injustice. You will find many similarities to the narrative method of 'A Tradition of Eighteen Hundred and Four'. There is one essential difference: the main narration is handed over to Selby in that story, but here the 1880s narrator tells the whole tale. However, he is clearly an "ear witness" to the events: there are references to "Phyllis used to say…" and so on. We feel that he *knows* the story, rather than *inventing* it, and the fiction is therefore thoroughly convincing.

Lovers

The final sentence, only three words long, obviously requires a third-person narrator. What effect do the final three paragraphs have as a conclusion to the love story?

The army

Soldiers

Hardy is at pains to create an **authentic historical picture**, but, if you have not studied 18th–19th-century history, you may find it confusing. Why are German soldiers on the South Coast of England? The note on **Soldiers** in the *Who's Who* section explains the wars against France and George III's German troops. It is, in fact, worse for Matthaus and Christoph than for many of these recruits. These two unwarlike young men are barely German at all. The Saarland and Alsace, their homes, are on the borders with France and have both been the subjects of territorial disputes: in fact, Alsace today is a part of France and the Saarland was administered by France until as recently as 1957. The hussars' distaste for war against France is understandable.

A love story

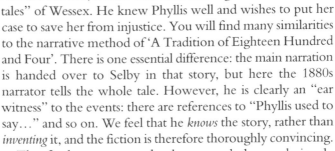

> **Love**
> There is much pressure, but Phyllis makes a choice: she *"decided to join"* Matthaus; she *"was inclined to follow"* Humphrey; she *"changed her mind"* and *"held on to her resolve."*

The story is focused entirely on Phyllis and Matthaus: it is told from Phyllis' point of view and Matthaus speaks at length about his feelings in Chapter 3. But what are these lovers really like?

Compare Phyllis' feelings in Chapter 2 with her behaviour in Chapter 5. Her first interest in Matthaus comes from pity as well as from her own wretched boredom: at the end of Chapter 2 she is still just "touched" and

Lovers

"interested". At the end of the story she shrieks at his death, nearly goes out of her mind and tends his memory for ever. Why then does she not go with him? Surely loyalty to Humphrey (whom she hardly knows) cannot explain it. The paragraph in Chapter 4 beginning "Phyllis was so conscience-stricken…" does much to explain why she chooses to stay, while that beginning "How Phyllis got through the terrible ordeal…" suggests how close she comes to changing her mind.

Professions

Phyllis is a dutiful member of the **bourgeoisie** (middle classes), the daughter of an intolerant, unsociable man, but still a doctor (so seen as a respectable professional). Humphrey approaches her through her father and the marriage is seen as a good match for her – a member of an old county family honouring the bourgeoisie. As a woman, Phyllis' position in society is vulnerable: she is dependent on her father or husband. Her father, always thoughtlessly cruel, eventually abuses his power by banishing her to her aunt's. This drives her to agitation and recklessness, but the sight of the returning Humphrey is enough to remind her of her "duty".

Soldiers

Matthaus Tina appears as a romantic figure, but his speech is not usually very passionate. Phyllis is to him part of the world he loves and respects, as distinct from the hated world in which he must live. Read Chapter 3, concentrating on the brief conversation when Phyllis is late and the next meeting when he proposes the escape. Look at the objects of his love. Phyllis ("my beloved", "meine Liebliche") is only one of the good things that save him from suicide: the words "dear", "devoted" and "passionate" are used, but not about Phyllis.

Lovers

This is typical of a Hardy love story in its depiction of unhappy lovers. All five love stories in *Wessex Tales* deal with the trials of love, with only one (somewhat false) happy ending. The moods of the stories differ, however. Think about 'The Melancholy Hussar'. Is it dramatic and exciting, moving and sad, or both? Is the ending tragic? Does it point to a moral?

The reader's sympathy

Certainly there is no doubt where the reader's sympathy lies. The sufferings of Phyllis and Matthaus would be enough to engage our sympathy, anyway, but there are further reasons. In many ways, the innocence and goodness of the central characters give the story much of its melancholy appeal. Look at the last paragraph of Chapter 3, explaining Phyllis's pure love for the "virtuous and kind" young German, or at Matthaus's simple loyalty to Christoph: "I cannot break faith with my friend". Then contrast this attitude with the ways in which Dr Grove (bullying and insensitive) and Humphrey Gould (thoughtless and equally insensitive) abuse their power over the dependent Phyllis.

Our sympathy for Phyllis and Matthaus is increased by Hardy's use of chance and irony. He frequently uses chance to set up coincidences which lead his characters to tragedy. He uses irony when characters act on misguided information and produce the opposite effect to that intended.

Chance

Irony and misunderstanding

Phyllis hears: "She has been in my mind these last two days much more than I should care to confess to everybody." Surely, she thinks, Humphrey intends to marry her?

In this story, Phyllis believes that Humphrey has lost interest in her and decides to escape with Matthaus. By a remarkable coincidence, she sees the returning Humphrey whilst on her way to Matthaus. His words to his friend are cleverly capable of two meanings: what is his "handsome peace-offering" making peace for? She lets Matthaus go on his own: he is captured and executed whilst she stands at the lovers' meeting-place watching in horror. The reader somehow feels that Phyllis' change of mind brought Matthaus and Christoph to this end. But is she really responsible for their deaths? Do they die because she delays them? Did the scheme ever have a hope of success? Is it possible to see Matthaus Tina as a victim not of love or chance, but of a cruel system, his noble sense of honour (not letting Christoph down, accepting guilt after capture) and a faulty navigational sense? Does chance save Phyllis's life? And for what?

The Withered Arm

Mr Lodge, a prosperous farmer, marries a beautiful young bride, Gertrude. Rhoda Brook, whom Lodge loved and deserted, leaving her with their son (now aged twelve) takes an unhealthy interest in Gertrude but refuses to see her. In a nightmare a vision of Gertrude, ugly and cruel, comes to Rhoda and she throws it off desperately. By degrees the two women get to know each other and Rhoda is shocked to find that Gertrude, in reality sweet and gentle, has suffered a gradual withering of the arm which coincides exactly with Rhoda's actions in the nightmare. They pay a visit to Conjuror Trendle who reveals Rhoda as the enemy who has cursed Gertrude. Rhoda leaves the area and six years pass. Gertrude suffers increasingly from her disfigurement and the neglect of her husband. In desperation she again seeks the advice of Trendle who advises her that her only chance is to touch the neck of a newly hanged man. This she does, only to find that Lodge and Rhoda are present: it is their son who has been hanged. Gertrude collapses and later dies.

A tale of the macabre

This is among the best known and most popular of Hardy's stories. It was first published in *Blackwood's Magazine*, which specialised in tales of the mysterious and the supernatural.

Mystery

The central mystery is the incident of the **incubus** – an evil spirit appearing in a nightmare. It is convincing owing to the power and economy of the writing at the time of its appearance: Rhoda being certain that it really is there and the simple question–and–answer passage with the boy about the noise in the "chimmer" (chamber, bedroom). When afflicted with the withering of her arm, Gertrude is at first relatively unconcerned, but another question–and–answer interlude fills Rhoda with guilt and dread.

The supernatural
Hardy does not commit himself to belief, but "they" (the whole community) speak of Trendle in the sort of terms you would use of "some medical man".

Tradition

The whole story is filled with the supernatural, the macabre and the the bizarre. Sometimes it is the power of **traditional belief**: Rhoda is assumed to be a witch, while the powers of Conjuror Trendle are widely trusted, though definitely not by Farmer Lodge who thinks himself and Gertrude too educated for such things. Hanging brings out more than one superstition: the "turning of the blood", for example, or buying bits of the rope as charms.

Chance

The emphasis on the macabre is increased by making **Gertrude**, who is young, town-bred and rather timid, the character to experience the terrifying rituals. In the end she cannot cope physically or mentally with the final, brutal touch of the macabre – not, in this, case an example of the supernatural, but occurring when chance dictates that the hanged man should be none other than Lodge's son. This is one of Hardy's most powerful coincidences – shocking, but perfectly possible. After all, one of the reasons for Gertrude being able to go to Casterbridge is Lodge's "business" away from home.

Finally, if we are inclined to treat everything as foolish, rustic superstition, we should note that not only are there several references in the story to the success of Trendle's remedy for epilepsy and skin complaints, but Hardy's Preface also suggests that the story has some factual basis.

Structure

The introduction to the *Wordsworth Classics* edition refers to this story as a "substantial novella". That opinion is clearly based on its nine chapters and six-year time-span, but is not really justified by other features of the story. Like many of the *Wessex Tales* it is the story of a relationship between two people; all the other characters are relatively shadowy. Write down all you learn about **Farmer Lodge** or his and Rhoda's son and see how little detail Hardy

Mystery

gives of them. **Conjuror Trendle** and the **hangman** are effective agents of the macabre, excellent in increasing the sense of mystery and the unknown, but not really engaging the reader's interest as characters.

The chapters, each with a title, are frequently brief "snapshots" of one event or scene. Do you think you could tell this story in nine drawings (or descriptive sentences), one for each chapter? If you attempt this, you are likely to find two things: the setting constantly changes and the events form themselves into visually dramatic **tableaux** (pictures).

Structurally, there is a division at approximately halfway through the tale (after Chapter 5): six years pass and the characters and type of story change.

Rhoda and Gertrude

'The Withered Arm' is the sort of tale to make your flesh creep, but the fact

Lovers

that it is much more than that owes a great deal to Hardy's characterisation of the two women.

Once again, two **lovers** are at the centre of the story – but they are not lovers of each other. The two women both win and lose the affection of Farmer Lodge. They occupy traditional roles at the start of the story: the faded, neglected ex-lover and the blooming young wife, divided by age, beauty, status and social class. However, in the first part of the story (Chapters 1–5) they act untypically and unselfishly.

Men and women

"Everything like resentment at the unconscious usurpation had quite passed away from the elder's mind."

Examine **Rhoda Brook's** attitude to the new Mrs Lodge as she sends her son out to report on her in Chapters 1 and 2, and decide which of the following words can be applied to her: obsessed; malicious; jealous; generous; hateful. Then turn to the opening paragraphs of Chapter 3 and the choice of words in Rhoda's nightmare visitation. Words like "maddened" and "desperate" are applied to Rhoda; words like "mockingly" and "cruelly" are applied to the vision of Gertrude. You can find many more similar examples. From these unpromising beginnings a relationship develops. Rhoda appears as helpless and therefore guiltless, though her brooding on Gertrude seems to have called up the incubus. Her reaction at the end of Chapter 3 sums her position up perfectly: "Can it be that I exercise a malignant power over people against my own will?"

If Rhoda is not a stereotypical "witch", then **Gertrude** is modest and considerate, lacking the vanity and self-conceit we might expect from her character. The boy, a keen observer, gives evidence of this: read the paragraph about her "silver-coloured gownd" for a beautifully under-stated contrast of modesty and vanity. Remind yourself of why she takes an interest in the boy and why she visits the cottage. The tentative, but genuine, friendship that grows in the first half masks the underlying tension of Rhoda's secret, shared only by the reader. The turning point in their relationship is understated, with no explosion of anger as Gertrude discovers her enemy but simply a tense constraint from Mrs Lodge and the later disappearance of Rhoda and her son.

Lovers

The **second half** is a different type of story. While the first half is about a relationship, the second describes a **quest**. Gertrude becomes the second victim of the superficial farmer's tendency to judge by appearances. His love was always based partly on pride in her appearance; now she feels neglected. In the first half Rhoda was obsessed by Gertrude's beauty; now Gertrude herself is obsessed by it as she tries to regain it. From being a "rosy-cheeked, tisty-tosty little body" (a tisty-tosty was a ball made of flowers), she has aged beyond her years.

Tradition

What other changes can you find in Gertrude Lodge after six years? Has her attitude to rustic traditions changed? In Chapter 3 the author remarks that "there was more of the strength that endures" in Rhoda than in "the soft-cheeked young woman before her". Does the end of the story confirm this view?

Verbal and visual: the power of the scene

It has already been suggested that you can emphasise the plot and impact of this story by a series of pictures, one per chapter; certainly, the power of 'The Withered Arm' is derived from a series of **set scenes**. This impact is created by both visual and verbal effects.

Let us look at **Chapter 8, A Waterside Hermit**. The structure of the **gallows** seems to dominate the whole chapter. Gertrude sees it in the second paragraph, then it is echoed in the wooden steps at the end of the executioner's cottage. Gertrude's last sight in the chapter is of the hangman climbing his steps. When she is at the house, the jail, with the condemned man behind his little window, looms over them. The conversation is full of telling details. Note how the tender-hearted Gertrude has changed through self-obsession to the point where she hopes there will be no reprieve and calls the yet-living

Professions

man "it". Davies, the hangman, while proud of his profession ("officer of justice"), is really a jobbing gardener. His speeches to Gertrude are full of irony as he is moved to help her by her attractive appearance ("I don't mind stopping a minute for such a one as you") although it is her deformed appearance that has brought her there.

See if you can pick out the visual and verbal details in other key scenes, for example:

- the first sight of Gertrude (Chapter 2);
- the first visit to Conjuror Trendle (Chapter 5);
- the scene in the jail after the execution (Chapter 9).

Irony and circumstance

Irony and misunderstanding

Compare Rhoda's actions towards Gertrude in Chapter 9 to those in Chapter 3 which she tries to put right – and that is why Hardy includes Gertrude here, to be attacked again.

Irony works in many ways, but the concept of **opposites** is always present: you may work very hard to achieve something but eventually achieve the

Chance

opposite; make an escape only to expose yourself to greater danger; or simply say the opposite of what you mean. The coincidence at the end is full of irony, with Rhoda, who attempted to cure Gertrude's deformity, playing a part in killing her. But you should also consider the ironies involved in such elements as:

- the relationship between Gertrude and the boy (compare Chapter 3 with Chapters 8 and 9);
- Lodge's reasons for marrying;
- Rhoda's intentions and achievements in Chapters 3-5.

Tradition and the past

Tradition

Uniquely in *Wessex Tales*, the opening of this story does not date it at some time in the past, but later references place it in the 1820s. This is useful in several ways. The old-fashioned **rustic characters** (well described in Chapter 1) help us to believe in the supernatural through their total belief and acceptance. Setting the story in the early years of the 19th century helps us to accept such "primitive" customs as the turning of the blood. It is also important that the condemned man should be seen as a

Wessex

victim. If Rhoda Brook had brought up a murderer, that would disturb the balance of the story, but the laws of the time saw rick-burning as a capital offence. Finally, the last pages give us a perspective on the lives of the main characters, with a memorable image of Rhoda just where she was at the beginning of the story.

◼ Self-test questions

'The Three Strangers', 'A Tradition of Eighteen Hundred and Four', 'The Melancholy Hussar of the German Legion', 'The Withered Arm'

Who? What? Why? When? Where? How?
1 Who lives beside a cart-track, deep in Egdon Heath?
2 What bears the inscription "THERE iS NO FUN UNTiLL i CUM"?
3 Why are Shepherd and Shepherdess Fennel celebrating?
4 When do Matthaus and Christoph die?
5 Where do two footpaths cross at right angles?
6 How does Gertrude Lodge discover that Rhoda Brook has cursed her as an enemy?
7 Who recognises Napoleon?
8 What does Gertrude wear on her first visit to church?
9 Why does Phyllis Grove change her mind about fleeing with Matthaus?
10 When was Casterbridge Gaol built?
11 Where, according to Solomon Selby, did Napoleon plan to land in England?
12 How does the hangman reveal his occupation to the party at Higher Crowstairs?

Who said… about whom?
1 "…she's a rosy-cheeked, tisty-tosty little body enough."
2 "He's a watch and clock-maker."
3 "The like o' that man's coolness eyes will never again see!"
4 "I think he lives with his mother a mile or two off."
5 "…she deserves it. I've treated her rather badly."
6 "I cannot break faith with my friend."

Open quotations
Identify and complete the following:
1 "Her hair is lightish, and her face…"
2 "What woman would not be pleased…"
3 "Here stretch the Downs, high and breezy and green…"
4 "The smile was neither mirthful nor sad…"
5 "…so as when I raise en up and hit my prisoner…"

Key sentences
The following sentences all occur at key points in the stories. Identify where they are.
1 "But at that moment a second shriek rent the air of the enclosure."
2 "A moment more and he had turned, closed the door, and fled."
3 "No sooner had this happened than Uncle Job gasped, and sank down as if he'd been in a fit."
4 "As the volley resounded there arose a shriek from the wall of Dr Grove's garden, and some one fell down inside."
5 "[she] whirled it backward to the floor, starting up herself as she did so with a low cry."

You should be able to deduce from the above examples one of Hardy's methods for increasing the drama and/or horror of key moments in the stories.

Prove it!

1. It is often suggested that Hardy writes only of the "common folk" of Wessex. Find three characters in these stories who could be described as professional or prosperous.
2. There are two executions (one a double one) and one scheduled execution in these stories. Can you find evidence to prove what feelings Hardy had about capital punishment and the people who carry it out?
3. Many characters in these stories choose a solitary life. Identify as many different reasons as you can for living in this way.

■ Text commentary

Fellow-Townsmen

The fellow-townsmen are Barnet, a businessman and town councillor, and Downe, a solicitor. Barnet is disastrously married to a social-climbing wife who has no time for him, while Downe is blissfully married to a sentimentally devoted wife. Barnet's previous love, Lucy Savile, whom he now regrets abandoning, still lives nearby. The plot turns on Mrs Downe's kind attempt to befriend Mrs Barnet: the boat in which the two ladies are sailing capsizes, Mrs Downe is drowned and Charlson, the disreputable surgeon, pronounces Mrs Barnet dead. Almost against his will Barnet revives her. Soon she leaves him and some months later dies. However, by the time he hears of this, Lucy, whom he has recommended to Downe as governess to his children, is about to marry her employer. Barnet leaves town, apparently for ever. His return 21 years later provides one last missed opportunity for him and Lucy, now a widow.

An urban tale

Of all the *Wessex Tales*, this is the one most firmly rooted in town life and, in the last chapter, the most modern in setting. All the characters have their place in the life of Bridport (Port Bredy), Barnet and Downe being identified as "fellow-burgesses" (citizens of a borough) on the first page. The first paragraph is a remarkable description of the small town enclosed by hills and pastures, but, though it depends on the surrounding country, it is a town in its own right. All the action takes place in the town, at its harbour a mile away and on the road between the two.

Professions

The action is essentially confined to the **middle classes** of the town, but within that the social position of each is clearly defined:

- **Mr Barnet** is a prosperous, first-generation gentleman, no longer really a businessman, but more respected because he does not have to work. His only social superior is his absurdly social-climbing wife who comes from London.
- **Mr Downe** is respectable – a working solicitor and a professional man – but Barnet's social inferior.
- **Lucy Savile** is also perfectly respectable, with artistic abilities; but she is not really an equal because of her poverty after the death of her naval officer father.

- **Charlson** is the disreputable professional – a man of ability, but one who cannot be trusted. At the beginning (Chapter 2) the mistrust of him is based on little more than his carelessness of convention.

Examine how these **class divisions** are revealed in the story. Look at the way in which people speak to each other: for example, among middle-class males of the time, the use of the surname on its own was less formal than "Mr". Observe also how class is expressed through the use of **servants** and, particularly, the different **dwellings** of the characters (and how changes in dwelling reflect changes in status). Chateau Ringdale is obviously the house most symbolic of class, but you should consider the other houses as well.

How many love stories?

Lovers

Like 'The Distracted Preacher', this story falls into the category of **novella**. The action covers 22 years as well as Barnet's "past" – the story of his love for Lucy and his foolish decision to put social ambition before his feelings and Lucy's merits – which is revealed in tantalising glimpses. The larger scale of this story is also suggested by the number of characters who are solidly drawn and have key decisions to make. Despite one or two dramatic incidents, this is definitely a character-based story.

Men and women

Two wives' hopes: "I hope you are not hurt, darling!" and "She... hopes you will excuse her joining you this evening."

Though involving only two men and three women, there are four significant male-female relationships among the main characters. Three can be defined fairly simply, though they are presented with great narrative vigour:

- **Downe and the first Mrs Downe** idealise married love. Find a scene which reveals this.

- **The Barnets** represent the complete collapse of a loveless marriage, mainly caused by Mrs Barnet. How many words does Mrs Barnet speak directly to her husband? What effect do you think Hardy intends?

- The married life of **Downe and Lucy** is not shown. Their marriage is a striking narrative device. It also poses questions about the permanence of Downe's devotion to his first wife. Together with the shrinking monument (the progress of which is worth following), it offers an astute and convincing picture of his emotional life.

Barnet and Lucy

Lovers

In the story of Barnet and Lucy, however, Hardy paints an unusually subtle picture of a loving relationship. It is a sad tale with which we sympathise, particularly when, at the end, the two middle-aged people are kept apart by nothing more than misunderstanding each other and a certain modest shyness. Barnet feels that he has done enough to spoil Lucy's life and accepts her rejection as final with a good grace. Lucy takes time to accustom herself to the surprise, is too respectable to dash off to the Black Bull and so loses her chance. As a result, Barnet is banished from his home town as well as from Lucy and she is left solitary in the house that symbolises much of both their lives, with only her step-daughters to keep her cheerful. The sad irony of their situation is that now no social barriers stand in their way and nobody will benefit from their parting.

Irony and misunderstanding

"I am a lonely old woman now…" "And I am a lonely old man", yet he accepts the gentlest of refusals and she takes two whole days to attempt contact with him.

Despite all this, we would be mistaken in seeing their relationship as a great passion thwarted. Barnet and Lucy are not passionate figures like Romeo and Juliet. The remarkable thing is that, in Chapter 9, Lucy is genuinely astonished that Barnet's departure was as a result of her marriage to Downe. The earliest meeting between them suggests a warm affection rather than a passion.

Love

"I must make the best of it, I suppose. But I shall never again meet with such a dear girl as you!" – hardly a passionate lover's farewell!

Barnet has managed to avoid her so well that, at the end of Chapter 1 (in response to his wife's coldness), he even wonders whether she still lives at the same place. Would he have thought of her at all if his wife had been even normally affectionate? In Chapter 2 he calls her "a dear girl" and Charlson uses the term "a nice little girl". That is how she is presented throughout: examine their meeting in Chapter 9 for signs of girlishness in the 45-year-old Lucy. Impulsive, honest and quick to show his feelings, Barnet accepts blame very readily in Chapter 2, but his claim that "it was destiny" that kept them apart does not carry conviction. Although there are elements of chance that

Chance

help to keep them apart, their separation is due to their own lack of will and confidence, together with their respect for convention and **middle-class morality**. At many times their actions do them credit, but they are not the actions of passionate lovers. In Chapter 5 we may be sure that Barnet's wife's death would have come as a blessing to him: observe his delight when she really dies. Yet he strives beyond his duty, for two and half hours after she has been taken from the water, and all his looks at Lucy's chimney count for nothing. Notice how the smoke from the chimney serves as a symbol of the progress of their love.

Chance

The one real blow that Fate ("the whimsical god... known as blind Circumstance") strikes at Barnet is a matter of timing. The Fates smile upon him in the death of his wife, he falls on his knees breathing "At last!" and then the servant delivers the other letter. Only now do Barnet's actions suggests a depth of passion: he tears the wallpaper and impulsively helps the sexton to tread in a stranger's grave. You should be able to find symbolic meaning in both those actions. It is, however, true that Barnet has given no sign of this passion previously. His behaviour towards Lucy is described as "almost paternal"; Lucy shows no guilt at the wedding because she has no idea of the depth of his feeling; and on hearing that Lucy is going to India after all, Downe acts while Barnet does not.

Lovers

Barnet is a subtly drawn character who is difficult to summarise. In the final chapter he shows no strong feelings, but appears "fearful of disturbing his own mental equilibrium"; he maintains the balance of his mind only by deliberate calm. You must make up your own mind about him. Is he a man with a great romantic passion which grows almost unnoticed within him and overwhelms him, making him a wanderer on the face of the earth? Or is he an impulsive man with plenty of money and too little to do whose indulgence of his own emotions allows Lucy to become an obsession? Or can you produce a better summary than either of these?

Time and change

Tradition

In many of the *Wessex Tales* we are given a picture of a world that seems unchanging: a non-industrial world with firmly rooted traditions. The narrator may tell us that things have changed by 1880, but the world of the stories still has an air of permanence and tradition. 'Fellow-Townsmen' is different. It is the most modern in feeling as well as in date, and change is all around. Examine Chapter 9 for signs of modernity in Port Bredy in the mid to late 1860s (note that the omnibus would be horse-drawn at this time).

Look again to find the things that have disappeared, decayed or aged: Barnet feels that the world of his younger days is no more. But Barnet himself has been an agent of change. In the meeting on the road (Chapter 1), an excellent introductory device typical of Hardy, we find a world in a state of change beneath the unchanging hills. Barnet has taken the first step towards becoming "old money": he no longer works for it as all his forebears have, but inherits it and pursues a life of leisure. The town itself is growing and establishing itself with a council, including Barnet. He, or rather his wife, is no longer content with the solid old family home, but wants to mimic the aristocracy. Barnet, and Port Bredy, are upwardly mobile – a progress that later sweeps Downe along with it.

Irony: Good deeds and Chateau Ringdale

Irony and misunderstanding

After Mrs Barnet leaves him: "It was for this that he had gratuitously restored her to life, and made his union with another impossible!"

In this story, Hardy uses irony in other forms than simple misunderstandings at crucial moments. Let us look at two of these forms. Whenever anyone attempts a good deed, its result is a personal disaster, often opposite to its intended effect. For instance, Downe, the happily married man, wishes to help his unhappily married friend, Barnet, by encouraging his wife to befriend Mrs Barnet. The result: Mrs Downe dies and Mrs Barnet leaves Barnet. Charlson, a selfish man, thinks of Barnet's interests in not trying too hard to revive his wife; Barnet, as a result, is more assiduous than ever the doctor would have been. What are the results of Barnet's good deeds? What comes of reviving his wife or of finding Lucy comfortable employment with Downe? There is no looming Fate in this story, but, as always with Hardy, any mortal who feels in control is deluding himself or herself.

Irony is also created by **Chateau Ringdale**, with its gloriously absurd, pretentious name. At the beginning, Barnet is too fond of peace for its own sake and his tolerance of his wife's scorn and neglect is cowardly rather than generous. But he does try to put his foot down over "Chateau Ringdale": not the unnecessary house, but the sign-board, named after a lord his wife once liked. Chateau Ringdale thus becomes a symbol of Mrs Barnet's ambition and selfishness. The irony lies in what becomes of it. Compare Chateau Ringdale in 1845 with Chateau Ringdale in 1866: whose character has it come to reflect? Find the sentence, "I believe it has been in the family for some generations" in Chapter 9 (said by the young man in the bookshop) and work out the layers of irony. Earlier, Chateau Ringdale becomes the scene for Barnet's meetings with Lucy: why is he there so often, even before he becomes used to her visits? The completion of the house should have been a social triumph for Mrs Barnet. Instead, what events dominate the occasion? This is a story of change, and the chateau is itself constantly changing in what it symbolises.

Terms of address: a note

You should already have looked at the difference in the ways Barnet and Downe address each other. Note also the **formality of address** used by all

the characters, with very respectable, middle-class overtones. Why should Lucy be the only character who is consistently addressed and referred to by her first name? There are at least three reasons, two of which have been mentioned in this commentary. Can you find Barnet's first name? Or Downe's? Try looking at Chapter 9, when suddenly reference is made to everyone's first names (except Charlson's). Is Hardy suggesting that the world has become less formal, or simply that the conventional, buttoned-up behaviour of the middle classes means less to Barnet now?

Interlopers at the Knap

Farmer Charles Darton, travelling to Kings Hintock with his groomsman (best man) Japheth Johns for the purpose of marrying Sally Hall, loses his way. Though he is delayed only a matter of hours, he arrives to find the situation complicated by another arrival. Sally's brother, Philip, has returned from Australia, poor, ragged, ill and with a wife and two children. Helena, his wife, is a former sweetheart of Darton who turned him down to marry Philip. When Philip dies that night and Darton wishes to assist Helena with the children, Sally insists on his marrying Helena, not her, which he does eighteen months later. The marriage is not particularly happy and Darton begins to think that he should have married Sally. Five years after her return from Australia, Helena dies and the story ends with Darton's three unsuccessful proposals to Sally, complicated by Japheth Johns proposing to her, too, and by misunderstandings about Darton's financial state. Sally remains single, and Darton remains puzzled, unable to understand her.

A comparison with 'Fellow-Townsmen'

The resemblances between these two stories are striking, in both their main plot and their details. The main story is of a prosperous man who has to make

Lovers

a choice between an intelligent, attractive, but unassuming young woman and one who appears to be of a higher class. He makes what appears to be the wrong choice of the "higher-class" woman, but is given a second chance by her death. His desire for the other woman increases with the years, but his final proposal is unsuccessful.

In terms of detail, you will immediately notice the opening: a scene-setting description of two men travelling together, discussing the qualities needed in a wife. The character and situation of Barnet and Darton have many resemblances – even their names sound similar. Both are prosperous, but they have not created their wealth. Their fathers built up the flax merchant's business and the farm; they themselves have either semi-retired or kept the farm ticking over. Each of them is kindly, but not good at understanding other people, especially women. In different ways, each is indecisive: Barnet follows impulses that drive him in different directions, while Darton takes too long to make up his mind.

It is strange that two stories which are so similar should produce such different effects. The main difference lies in the plots. In 'Fellow-Townsmen',

Chance

the superior story, there are coincidences and chance events, but the plot is driven by the characters and the decisions they (notably Barnet) make. In 'Interlopers at the Knap', the plot is more contrived, dominated by chance and coincidence. It is a perfectly reasonable use of chance to have Darton lose his way (the fact that he has not been there often may indicate the sort of courtship it has been) and therefore have an "interloper" arrive at the Knap (hill-top) before him. However, the coincidences pile up in Chapters 2 and 3:

- Darton proposed to Helena years before.
- He finds her in the stable the moment before Sally and her mother enter.
- Philip happens to meet the carrier and gives Helena Darton's present to Sally, a dress which she wears in an act that is both accidentally symbolic and confusing to Darton.
- An unexpected burst of rain and his need for sleep bring Darton and Helena together in the middle of the night.
- Philip conveniently dies.
- Sally enters with the news as Darton says, "You belong to another, so I cannot take care of you."

There is a definite sense of the author manipulating the storyline. You should be able to find similar uses of events in Chapter 5. Look at the various misunderstandings involving Japheth and the bank that prompt Darton to differing conclusions about the possibility of success with Sally.

Because of our comparative lack of involvement with Darton we react very differently at the end of this story from at the end of 'Fellow-Townsmen'. Re-read the last few pages of each tale (the final proposal and the behaviour of the characters afterwards) and ask yourself these questions:

Lovers
- What is the difference between the motives of Lucy and Sally?
- Which characters (if any) do we feel sorry for?
- Is it the "right" ending for the characters themselves?

Sally Hall

Men and women

Remind yourself of the first description of Sally: she is "handsome" but most of it tells of character – good nature, decision, judgement, warm-heartedness, quick spirits.

If Charles Darton is not among the most interesting male characters in *Wessex Tales*, then at least Sally Hall may be the most modern of the young women. The first reference to her comes in Chapter 1, in the paragraph beginning "Why I have decided to marry her…" as Darton explains that he has had enough of "superior women" since he has finished with "you know who I mean" (Helena, as we later realise). Darton misjudges his woman badly when he dismisses her as "simple" (Japheth Johns corrects him) and regards marriage as simply *his* decision. However, he is the first to make use of the key word for Sally:

independent. Her first speech (in Chapter 2) is delivered "independently".

Sally does not accept the dependent state of women in Victorian times. She refuses to worry about her fiancé's late arrival and is quite prepared to let him go if he is put off by her vagabond brother's return. Shaken by seeing Darton and Helena looking significantly at each other, she still takes charge of the children. Sally's independence is a decisive characteristic in the story. It can lead her either to act against her own interest or to do as she wishes despite the disapproval of others. Examine Sally's motives in the following key scenes:

Lovers

- the discovery of Darton and Helena when bringing the news of Philip's death;
- the Chapter 4 letter and her non-arrival with Helena just before;
- the final refusal of Darton's offer and other later offers.

One of the reasons for her refusal of offers of marriage is that she has come to realise that women need not always be dependent on men; she can live her life her own way. It is important to remember, however, that her attitude is coloured by the fact that she is not *financially* dependent on men, as so many Victorian women were. She is a rustic, unsophisticated, but far from unintelligent, version of the late 19th-century **New Woman**.

The letters

Most of the conversations in this story are very short: the longest is between Mrs Hall, Philip and Sally, and has to carry much narrative information as well as the grief and shock of mother and sister. The fact that three letters written by Sally are included gives the reader much more insight into her than into the other characters.

Men and women

"I will not try to explain what, in truth, I cannot explain – my reasons; I will simply say that I must decline to be married to you." Though the letter is friendly, Sally is decisive.

Examine the way in which she begins and ends her letters. Although the opening becomes more formal when she is no longer Darton's fiancée, she signs off in a more affectionate way in the later letters. Why should this be? The first letter (Chapter 4) is remarkably forthright, generous and fair and emphatic in style. In the third letter (Chapter 5) we see that she is genuinely his "faithful friend". He has looked after her nephew and niece and she is grateful, and delighted that his finances have not collapsed. Incidentally, she is indignant at the suggestion that her refusal may have some connection with his supposed collapse. But it is in her second letter that her character emerges best. Trying to refuse him in as kindly a way as possible whilst keeping her reasons to herself, she cannot resist a touch of affectionate satire at the expense of a man she has come to realise is anything but her superior. He may be very good with mangold-wurzels; it is just people that he doesn't understand.

Humour

Japheth Johns

Japheth Johns is one of the most successful rustic portraits in *Wessex Tales*: a dairyman, so not poor, but combining in himself the wisdom and simplicity of many of Hardy's rural characters, all expressed in vigorous, frequently comical dialect speech.

Rustics

Regional fiction

"She was a woman worth having if ever woman was. And now to let her go!", "Ah, Charles, you threw a prize away when you let her slip five years ago."

His wisdom is best shown in his appreciation of Sally Hall's excellent qualities of character. If you examine what he says about Sally in Chapters 1, 4 and 5, you will find a much greater understanding of her than his friend ever manages. He even falls out temporarily with Darton over his foolish choice of Helena as his wife. Japheth's own proposal to Sally occupies our (and Hardy's) attention and interest very briefly.

Japheth's main contribution to the story is **humour**. This is occasionally physical, like climbing the sign-post to find the route, but mostly verbal. It is a mistake to think of this form of verbal humour as just simply laughing at the quaintness of a simple man (though there is plenty of quaint vocabulary).

Humour

Imaginative and unexpected imagery creates as much humour, for example in his speech near the end of Chapter 1. There are not enough letters on the sign to show the way to "Smokeyhole" (Hell), a lively simile,

and this is followed by a fine flight of fancy when Japheth imagines that he is like Columbus exploring a land where the natives have lost the art of writing. His speech on the respective merits of cider and malt liquor in Chapter 3 is a gloriously solemn piece of nonsense. Choice of drink is treated

Wessex

as a family tradition, like religious or political beliefs, and his praise for cider as a peaceable drink is less than convincing: you may go a whole year without getting into a fight! Make as long a list as you can of

Japheth's individual use of the Wessex **dialect**. Many of the phrases (for example, "such a red-herring doll-oll-oll") are totally unfamiliar, but have obvious meaning.

The others

The other characters in the story are less well developed. **Mrs Hall** is sensible and sympathetic, conventional in seeing Darton as a good match, and tries with some success to cope with the change brought by Philip's return. **Philip** has a dramatic scene (one woe following another in a slow process), then dies without telling us what really happened in Australia. **Helena** receives fair treatment from the author: she previously left Darton for honourable reasons and her marriage to him is not the result of her scheming, but of poverty and Sally's willingness. However, we can see how little Hardy attempts to gain our interest for her by reading the section on her marriage and death in Chapter 4.

The effect of the story

What sort of a story do you think Hardy is writing here? Is it tragic, sad, humorous or serious, a story with a moral or a tale to enjoy for its twists of Fate? Is the story more important than the characters? Does the reader feel satisfaction at the ending?

The Distracted Preacher

Richard Stockdale, a young Methodist minister, takes temporary charge of the chapel in the village of Nether-Moynton. He is recommended to take lodgings at the house of Mrs Newberry, a widow. To his surprise Lizzy Newberry is young and attractive and soon he falls in love with her. She is clearly attracted to him, too, and she is usually attentive and frequently flirtatious. However, her behaviour is perplexing: even at their first meeting she cures his cold with brandy concealed in the church tower! Stockdale is extremely slow to realise that she is one of the leaders of a gang of smugglers; he is also worried about her intimacy with Jim Owlett, her cousin and confederate. Eventually Stockdale's infatuation and concern for Lizzy's safety lead him to the fringe of the smugglers in a highly eventful time when they land a fresh supply of brandy. They are discovered by the customs officers who confiscate the spirits, only for the smugglers to regain them in an ambush. Stockdale and Lizzy are both unprepared to change their lifestyles and he leaves for another part of the country. In an epilogue, two years later, Stockdale returns to Nether-Moynton, where Lizzy has fallen on hard times and Owlett has emigrated to America on the collapse of the smuggling trade. They marry and embark on a life of respectability.

Smugglers!

Tradition

An exciting yarn about smugglers may seem to be the stuff of adventure stories, but this novella is not like that. Admittedly there are atmospheric descriptions and exciting accounts of the smugglers at work as well as much humour, mainly at the expense of the "Preventives", but Hardy is at pains to make his story realistic. His Preface explains how much of the story comes either from oral tradition or from historical incident. In the story itself, the tradition of smuggling as a "normal" activity is stressed. Nether–Moynton clearly operates its own standards of **morality**: in the first two pages we find that many of the villagers attend both church and chapel to be on the safe side (and not to miss the tea) and that it seems quite normal for Mrs Newberry to refuse to take "government folks".

Regional fiction

"My father did it, and so did my grandfather, and almost everybody in Nether-Moynton lives by it, and life would be so dull if it wasn't for that, that I should not care to live at all."

Smuggling is a traditional family business for the Simpkins, Newberry and Owlett families. In Chapter 4 the first man Lizzy meets when she goes out to "burn off" the ship is "one of the most devout members" of Stockdale's congregation; nine of the carriers are also members of his congregation and the vicar is a good customer. There is an alternative morality in Nether-Moynton: these people are not bad or corrupt, but they simply do not see smuggling as wrong. Their treatment of the outnumbered customs men in the ambush, an excellent example of their lack of cruelty, is based on historical fact (see Hardy's Preface). What justification does Lizzy Newberry give for smuggling? Does Hardy seem to sympathise with it? Do you find his view convincing?

A mystery?

Is this story an example of a mystery story? It has various trademarks of the type: a stranger comes to town and encounters a beautiful, mysterious woman whose actions puzzle him until one night he confronts her and, to his horror,

Mystery

finds the truth. But, in fact, the biggest mystery is why Stockdale takes so long to realise the truth. His innocence is one of the story's narrative strengths. It is always amusing and flattering to read a story in which the reader is several steps ahead of the central character. Some of the smugglers' tricks are indeed mysterious (the apple-tree, for instance), but Lizzy's occupation is obvious from the moment she takes Stockdale to the tower, finds the tubs and shows thorough knowledge of the smuggling trade, even down to adulterating the liquor. Her strange hours of sleeping and rising, the brushing of the coat, the spy in the tree and other clues are still not enough to convince Stockdale and he believes her unconvincing stories of limited involvement. Halfway through Chapter 4 he finally says, "You are a smuggler." Make a list of all the evidence necessary for him to reach the conclusion you reached in Chapter 1.

Humour

Humour

In fact, the mystery is more a source of humour than of anxiety. Lizzy's excuses – for example, she's not really dressed as a man because she has her dress on underneath – and Stockdale's attempts to find moral justification (it's all right to drink the smuggled brandy so long as you don't add water to deceive the buyer) are equally far-fetched.

The attempts of the customs men to solve the mystery are, for the most part, comical. In particular, Chapter 6 finds Hardy enjoying himself at the expense of **Latimer** and the customs men. Even the title, 'The Great Search at Nether-Moynton', is mock-heroic, pretending to greatness for comic effect, as is the phrase "Latimer and his myrmidons", comparing them to the war-like followers of the Greek hero Achilles. The lists of places searched provide a vivid picture of a day that steadily gets worse. Compare the three lists: "mixens", by the way, are dung-heaps. No wonder three of them have lost their sense of smell! The way the lists are set out on the page is unusual: what effect does Hardy obtain by this?

Rustics

The behaviour of the smugglers themselves adds to the humour. When the Methodist preacher joins them in the tower, Jim Clarke worries that it might lose them the trade of the Church of England parson. Lizzy's disabling of the carts and Hardman, the blacksmith, poking his head out of the holly bush at the wrong moment could both provide visual humour in a film farce. The attack on the Preventives is also not to be taken seriously, with the huge females, the undamaged customs men and Latimer's change from valour to discretion once freed. The reader accepts Lizzy's view that nobody is harmed by smuggling; the smugglers themselves are safe because Latimer's men are so incompetent, even though saturation coverage of the village gains them temporary possession of the brandy.

The last page, an **epilogue** though not labelled as such, reveals the truth – that smuggling is dangerous – but that is not the impression given during the story. There are, of course, some exciting scenes, like Lizzy "burning off" the ship (lighting fires to warn of the presence of customs men). However, despite the excitement and the growing concern of Owlett and Lizzy at Latimer's persistence, it remains something of a game, with the smugglers controlling play. Even when the spirits are found, the emergency plan slides smoothly into action: Lizzy is to "look to the linch-pins and screws" and "the chaps will do the rest".

A love story

Love

Stockdale's attempts at correct behaviour are doomed. He begins by calling Lizzy "Mrs Newberry", then "Lizzy" and "dear Lizzy" before reaching his hopeless infatuation with "my dear Lizzy."

Rather than a tale of smugglers or a mystery, 'The Distracted Preacher' is another of Hardy's stories of ill-assorted lovers. It is a tale of innocence on both sides. Stockdale is supremely innocent – innocent of Lizzy's feminine wiles as much as of her involvement in smuggling. Lizzy's innocence is of the normal moral standards: she does not understand that most people would disapprove of smuggling as a crime.

Lovers

This is by no means the only story in which Hardy makes the woman a much stronger character than the man. Sally Hall in 'Interlopers at the Knap' is frequently described as "independent"; surely Lizzy is even more so. Examine the characters of Sally and Lizzy, comparing the forms that their independence takes: their opinions, decisions, actions and ways of life.

Men and women

You might like to make the point that Lizzy literally "wears the trousers" at times. But, when accused of wearing men's clothes, she falters and shrinks – untypically timid behaviour.

Lizzy is also a stronger character because of the **balance** of their feelings for each other. In the first four pages, Stockdale is described as "a lonely young fellow who had for weeks felt a great craving for somebody on whom to throw away superfluous interest and even tenderness". He is ready to fall in love. Lizzy, "a fine and extremely well-made young woman", has "eyes that warmed him before he knew it". What chance does he have? Remember that Lizzy's abrupt changes of behaviour are due largely to having to lie about smuggling, but also in part to teasing Stockdale and maintaining power over him. In Chapter 1, look at the matter of the chicken for tea and compare Stockdale's attempt at sophistication with Lizzy's control of the situation. Still in the same chapter, note how easily she controls his actions: previously he would have disapproved of drinking alcohol, never mind sneaking into the church to fetch smuggled liquor.

Professions

Richard Stockdale, in truth, is a fairly unlikely Methodist minister. There are two reasons for this. He is, of course, extremely young (described as "a very lovable youth") and as impressionable as he is moral. Secondly, he is a "distracted preacher". "Distracted" can mean "made mad" or "led off course". He is not mad but infatuated and so distracted from what he should do. He wishes to be good, and is good, but sometimes has to use dubious reasoning to persuade himself that what he is doing is moral. In rescuing the customs men then leaving the village when Lizzy refuses to give up smuggling and marry him, he finally asserts his Christian morality.

In the same way, Lizzy is less in control in the later stages. Her flirtatious confidence in dealing with Stockdale is replaced by open talk of her love for him, tears at their parting and a symbolic glistening pane of glass for her last sighting of him. She is still in many ways the same Lizzy, however – bold, independent and adventurous. Read her speech a few pages from the end, in the paragraph beginning "But why should you belong to that profession?"

Professions

Then we come to the problem of the final page – the **epilogue**. Everything has changed. The changes in Stockdale are perfectly predictable: he is much more like a professional minister. But what of the changes in Lizzy? "I own (admit) that we were wrong," she says: does this sound like the independent-minded Lizzy Newberry? Why has she so changed? The customs officers now have "blood-money" for capturing or killing smugglers – enough to make Latimer efficient? Owlett is in America and, in an unrelated sadness, Lizzy's mother has died.

This story makes almost no use of **chance** – the events are generated by the characters. At the end, however, chance is used to pile disasters on Lizzy. She even writes a book called *Render unto Caesar*, the title taken from the passage in St Matthew's Gospel which Stockdale quoted to her in Chapter

Chance
4 (and received the splendid retort, "He's dead"). In the passage the Pharisees try to trick Jesus into a revolutionary comment, asking him about the taxes they have to pay to Rome (of which Caesar is the Emperor). Christ replies, "Render unto Caesar the things that are Caesar's" – in other words, pay your taxes. Now Lizzy warns people off crime, with a Biblical quotation as her title.

Men and women

When considering the change in Lizzy, note that she "studied" her duties with "praiseworthy assiduity". This sounds like a school report: her behaviour is learned rather than natural.

Why does Lizzy change so completely? Is this ending convincing? Read Hardy's note at the end of the story. Why do you think it was *de rigueur* (essential, insisted upon) in the nineteenth century for the story to end with Lizzy's marriage to Stockdale?

This was not the only problem Hardy had with Victorian morality in magazine censorship: various of his novels were altered when serialised to suit the tastes of the magazine readers. The note (which writes of them as if they really existed) suggests that Lizzy should have married Jim Owlett. Would the story be improved by making that change? Do you think that Hardy would have written the whole story differently if it was to end with the marriage of Lizzy and Jim? To help you make up your mind, check the references to Owlett in the story, looking for any signs of Lizzy's caring for him or of Stockdale's jealousy. Does Hardy build in enough indication of Owlett's relationship with his cousin? Whatever decision you make about the most suitable ending for the story, one thing is certain: Hardy did not really believe in the ending imposed on him. In a story which examines human relationships with subtlety, affection and humour, the ending is sudden and abrupt. There is just time for a sly joke at Stockdale's expense ("a few powerful sentences of his own").

Church and chapel

With a preacher as one of the central characters, it is important to understand the differences between the two churches referred to. Some of the terms are now rather out of date. The first paragraph uses the terms "Wesleyan" and "Methodist" in relation to Stockdale's congregation. Later the term "Dissenter" is used. **Methodism** (the only one of those terms still regularly used) was founded by John Wesley and, like all the Nonconformist churches, dissented from (disagreed with) the Church of England. The terms "Wesleyan" and "Dissenter" are used here with the same meaning. The **Episcopalians** referred to are members of the Church of England. Until recently, Methodist churches were referred to as "chapels": hence those "trimmers" who went to church with the vicar (or parson) in the morning and to chapel with Stockdale in the evening. Stockdale's problems are increased by the fact that Methodism lays greater stress on personal moral responsibility than most churches: he is not allowed "tutelary (protective) saints" to look after him in moments of weakness.

Professions

Will Latimer

Will Latimer is a traditional figure of fun, the pompous authority figure who is stupid enough to bring disaster on himself and expose himself to ridicule.

It should not be difficult to analyse the **humour** generated by Latimer and his customs men. Most of it comes from character and from visual jokes. One of Latimer's problems is that there is a large difference between how he sees himself and how he really is. He thinks that it is impressive to ride round on a white horse; Lizzy thinks it is easy to see him at night when he wants to be secret. He knows that he will get the better of these smugglers and, indeed, eventually finds the liquor; Lizzy quietly disables all the carts and he is stupid enough to appeal to her for assistance. Examine the humour in the following sections:

Humour

- the hunt in Chapter 6 where Latimer loses all the villagers;
- the conversations with Lizzie and Hardman at the beginning of Chapter 7;
- his behaviour later in the same chapter when Stockdale rescues him.

The only problem for the reader is reconciling this blundering buffoon with the deadly customs men who appear in the epilogue.

A Wessex tale

This tale sums up perfectly Hardy's use of the Wessex setting in his fiction. The humour of **dialect** and the importance of **tradition** we have encountered previously, though Hardy's use of tradition (smuggling and alternative morality) is especially important here. The impact of the stranger is also typical of small communities. But what is unusual in 'The

Wessex

Distracted Preacher' is the use that Hardy makes of his intimate knowledge of local geography.

Many events are dependent on the Wessex terrain: the chases, the ambush, the switch from one landing-place to another. Nether-Moynton becomes almost a character in its own right and the large town of Budmouth appears as an unreachable sanctuary for the floundering Latimer.

Regional fiction

Notice the way in which characters and objects disappear into the landscape: even Latimer's men end up as "voices from a thicket"!

■ Self-test questions

'Fellow-Townsmen', 'Interlopers at the Knap', 'The Distracted Preacher'

Who? What? Why? When? Where? How?
1 Who made a sampler at the age of eleven?
2 What does Andrew Jones do for a living?
3 Why did Helena marry Philip Hall, instead of Charles Darton?
4 When does Barnet's wife leave him?
5 Where are the tubs of brandy that Latimer and his men find?
6 How does Owlett disguise himself in the ambush on the customs men?
7 Who lives briefly in America, Australia, India and the Cape (South Africa)?
8 What does Philip take at the Sow and Acorn and give to Helena?
9 Why does Susan Wallis visit Lizzy Newberry?
10 When does Lizzy go to chapel?
11 Where is the White Horse Inn?
12 How many church-goers are there in Nether-Moynton; how many chapel-goers; how many people altogether?

Who said... about whom?
1 "You must be happy if any man is."
2 "I shouldn't call [her] simple."
3 "He's neither for nor against us. He'll do us no harm."
4 "He always rides a white horse."
5 "She was a treasure beyond compare."
6 "You dissent from Church and I dissent from State."

Open quotations
Identify and complete the following:
1 "She no longer belongs to another..."
2 "...he did not want the chicken, unless..."
3 "She did wait – years and years –, but..."
4 "I want something more striking – more like..."
5 "Nine of 'em are..."

Key sentences
The following all occur at key points in the stories. Identify where they are.
1 "The triangular situation – himself-his wife-Lucia Savile – was the one clear thing."
2 "Then, almost involuntarily, Barnet fell down on his knees and murmured some incoherent words of thanksgiving."
3 "It was the first meal that they had ever shared together in their lives, and probably the last that they would so share."
4 "She interposed with a stout negative, which closed the course of his argument like an iron gate across a highway."
5 "On the evening of the 1st of March he went casually into his bedroom about dusk, and noticed lying on a chair a greatcoat, hat, and breeches."

What do these incidents have in common as key points in the stories?

Prove it!
1 "Hardy's main male characters can be seen as ineffectual lovers." Do you think that this is fair comment? Find the evidence to support your view.
2 Is it fair to describe the rustic characters as simple? What evidence is there to support and contradict that view?
3 The settings of these three stories are very different, though all are in Wessex. How are the stories appropriate to their settings?

■ How to write a coursework essay

Many of you will use your study of *Wessex Tales* as part of a Wide Reading coursework assignment for GCSE English/English Literature. If we look at the requirements for the NEAB examinations, we find that this assignment must involve *comparison* between a complete pre-20th-century prose text and a suitable 20th-century text. It is also essential to make certain comments on the historical, social and cultural background to the texts. For this the stories of Hardy are particularly suitable, since the Wessex social background is such an important part of the literary effect. In the following pages we examine five possible subjects for Wide Reading assignments. Throughout the Text Commentary the **Essays icon** draws attention to useful material for these assignments.

There are, of course, some general principles for these assignments. **Comparison** is essential. No credit is given for telling the story of a Hardy tale and then that of a 20th-century novel on a vaguely similar theme. It is essential that you show that, while Hardy draws his characters, uses social background or organises his plots in such a way, D.H. Lawrence, for example, does it differently, identically or in a partly similar way. Therefore your choice of 20th-century comparison is important. There must be specific grounds for comparison. This can, of course, mean that the 20th-century story is opposite in effect from Hardy: using similar ideas differently is a good ground for comparison.

It is your own decision whether to use one Hardy story or several. Basing an essay on 'A Tradition of Eighteen Hundred and Four' would probably be foolish, but there is plenty of material for an essay in, for example, 'The Distracted Preacher'. However, it improves an essay to show a more general knowledge of Hardy's stories even if the main concentration is on only one.

The most important consideration when writing an essay is that it must develop an **argument** or explain a point of view consistently throughout. Choosing a **title** matters: if you write an essay called 'The Supernatural in Hardy and M.R. James', you are not directing yourself towards a specific comparison. The comparison should be made throughout the essay, not necessarily in the same sentence, but at least in adjacent paragraphs. You should make a decision on what each paragraph is about, as far as possible signalling this decision to the reader in the opening sentence. This is often called a **topic sentence** as it explains the topic or, as in this case, the stage in the argument of the paragraph.

In terms of **length** of essay, do bear in mind that it is only one of several pieces of coursework and there is no need for a 5,000-word blockbuster. Many essays will exceed 1,000 words; by how much depends on the material you wish to present and the advice of your teacher.

Men and women

Examine the extent to which the treatment of men and women in the short stories of Thomas Hardy and Margaret Atwood reflects their social and cultural background.

Margaret Atwood in many ways is as different from Hardy as is possible: not only female, but feminist, a Canadian academic born in 1939 as against a largely self-taught Wessex man born in 1840. The best approach to this essay would be to test the predictable differences against the actual stories. The collection of Margaret Atwood stories we are using is *Dancing Girls*, written in the 1970s and published in paperback by Vintage.

We might expect Hardy's stories to express the male point of view and to accept the inferior and vulnerable position of women in society. Is this true? Phyllis Grove is a victim of the need for respectability, but what about Lizzy Newberry and Sally Hall? We would certainly expect Atwood's stories to reflect women's sufferings and their need for independence. Julia in 'Lives of the Poets' fits into that pattern (lonely, isolated, with a man who is casually betraying her), but what is the balance of blame in stories like 'The Resplendent Quetzal' and 'The Grave of the Famous Poet'? Perhaps it's a matter of viewpoint – most of Atwood's stories are told from the female perspective and most of Hardy's from the male. Again, though, it is dangerous to generalise, most particularly in 'The Withered Arm', which is, in part, a love story and in which the man remains in the background. Atwood, on the other hand, can write 'Polarities', which centres on a female character, Louise, but in which the viewpoint is that of Morrison, her male colleague. In conclusion, you will be able to show many of the expected differences, but Hardy and Atwood are both outstanding short story writers who defy stereotyping.

Look also at the differences in social and geographical setting and narrative style. Atwood sets many stories on or around campus and has great skill in evoking drab places in the open spaces of Canada where nothing seems to happen. Her characters are often students, graduates and teachers. In her narrative Atwood concentrates more on the inner life of her characters. In 'Lives of the Poets' the plot is simply that Julia has a nosebleed shortly before a reading at an obscure university, thinks about her life, tries to phone home (Marika, the "other woman", answers) and waits to be taken to the reading. Perhaps you might find that her most striking "feminine" characteristic is her ability to empathise with characters and create fiction from their thoughts and emotions as much as from their actions. Does Hardy ever do this? You might like to consider the first half of 'The Withered Arm'.

The supernatural

What means does Hardy use to make the supernatural events in 'The Withered Arm' convincing? Compare these to the methods used by M.R. James in his Ghost Stories.

If you choose to write about the supernatural in *Wessex Tales*, you are limited in terms of detailed study to one story: 'The Withered Arm'. There is really only one essay title to choose with the supernatural. If a ghost story or a tale of evil spirits is convincing, it will make your flesh creep; if it is unconvincing, it will simply seem silly. The comparison we are making is with M.R. James, the most famous writer of ghost stories in his day (his stories were published between 1904 and 1931). His stories are available in the budget-priced Penguin Popular Classics. You may well prefer to write on some more modern writer of horror – the grounds for comparison remain the same.

Tales of the supernatural happen to people and it is the nature of these people that has the biggest effect on whether we believe the story. With Hardy it is the culture and sense of community that are all-important. You will have no trouble explaining Hardy's use of tradition (this is a chance to use other stories for background); part of that tradition is belief in the power of conjurors, the existence of evil spirits, the effectiveness of charms and so on. M.R. James uses the opposite method. We can be made to believe in the supernatural if everyone does, or if a sceptical character does. James specialises in knowledgeable academics who are forced to believe by painful experience, such as Professor Parkins in 'Oh, Whistle and I'll Come to You, My Lad' or Edward Dunning, the expert in alchemy, in 'Casting the Runes'. Of course, Hardy uses a converted sceptic as well as a believing community: what does Gertrude Lodge first say about Conjurer Trendle?

You will need to examine the ways in which the supernatural is made to seem real. The events need to happen to "real" people. The characters of Rhoda and Gertrude help us to believe in a way that M.R. James (and possibly the modern horror writers) cannot. A further key factor is the actual presentation of the supernatural (an area in which some of the modern writers are at their strongest). Hardy achieves much by making the events physically real to the people involved (Rhoda feels the spirit's arm after the nightmare), but avoiding too many objective details that could become absurd. This reaches its peak in Chapter 9, when the macabre horror and Gertrude's collapse are horribly realistic, but it is impossible to attribute anything certainly to supernatural means. In 'Oh, Whistle and I'll Come to You, My Lad' (probably the best example to choose for comparison), the supernatural events are channelled through the perceptions of the brave, but increasingly terrified,

Parkins. Both stories, though, use the device of objective corroboration, via characters such as Rhoda's son and the Colonel.

You might also like to consider the effect of the remote past in tales of the supernatural: James and Hardy are two of many writers to make use of ancient traditions and ancient artefacts in fostering belief.

Love

Several of Hardy's Wessex Tales deal with unhappy love affairs and the pressures that keep lovers apart. Compare Hardy's treatment of this theme with the love between Winston and Julia in George Orwell's 1984.

For this essay there is one essential strand of argument which can be developed in great detail. The main point of comparison is the degree to which the separation of the lovers is imposed from outside. In *1984* (available in Penguin paperback), the political system leaves Winston and Julia a choice only between deserting each other and risking torture and death. Another example you might want to choose instead of *1984* is *Across the Barricades* by Joan Lingard, which describes danger and outside pressure for young lovers caught in sectarian violence in Northern Ireland. You need to show that Thomas Hardy's lovers fail mainly as a result of their own choices. Perhaps the best stories to write about are 'The Melancholy Hussar' and 'Fellow-Townsmen'. Nearly all Hardy's lovers are ill-assorted: Matthaus is literally an outsider (like Stockdale in the only happily ending love story) while Barnet and Lucy suffer from class divisions – the social climate is against both sets of lovers. You will also have no trouble in finding examples of chance working against the lovers, usually in coincidences of timing. However, there are times in these stories when the characters have a choice and fail to act positively. In *1984*, on the other hand, what were social pressures in Hardy are replaced by a repressive totalitarian regime. Love becomes a political act. Unlike the Hardy heroes and heroines, the undoing of Winston and Julia is to act boldly.

You should emphasise the authors' attitude to society. Hardy is writing 60 years before Orwell, but looking back, whereas Orwell predicts the future. Do you think they share similar views on the individual in society?

You will also want to examine the lovers themselves. Where do you find the greater passion? Which is more important: love or life?

Regional fiction

Compare the effects of the use of regional background and customs in the short stories of Thomas Hardy and D.H. Lawrence.

For this essay you can choose to write on whichever stories you prefer: all the *Wessex Tales* make great use of regional background. It would probably be advisable to deal with at least three; otherwise generalisations will be dangerous. For comparison, the best Lawrence story to choose is probably 'Odour of Chrysanthemums', which can be found in many selections, including the budget-price Dover Thrift paperback. 'The Christening', in the same selection, might be useful; other good regional stories to be found elsewhere include 'Tickets, Please' and 'Strike Pay'.

You need first of all to be specific about the region: Lawrence is writing of the mining areas of Nottinghamshire and at a later date than Hardy. 'Odour of Chrysanthemums' was published in 1914 (not too long after *Wessex Tales*), but Lawrence does not look back in his settings to the extent that Hardy does. Both often deal with village and small town life, but there is a difference between agricultural and industrial society.

Although he spent portions of the year in London, Hardy was based in his native Dorset until his death; Lawrence moved away from the East Midlands which he viewed with a mixture of nostalgia and revulsion. This will give you the clue to many of the differences and points of comparison.

Wessex life can be restrictive and limiting, but Hardy also derives much affectionate humour from it: through village life in 'The Distracted Preacher', for instance, or from characters like Japheth Johns. Society is basically supportive, the locals generally live according to a moral code of which Hardy approves (and act in a Chorus role) and their dialect speech is full of vigour and humour. You will find no difficulty in discovering examples of rural society's limitations, but generally it has a benign influence. Lawrence's stories, on the other hand, emphasise the harshness of work: the physical state of the former miner, old Rowbotham, in 'The Christening' or the death of Bates in 'Odour of Chrysanthemums'. This harshness brutalises the men, for example in young Rowbotham's coarse mockery or Bates' drinking. Lawrence, like Hardy, makes great use of dialect, but it is frequently ugly. Often Lawrence's sympathy is with the outsider: a woman in a male-dominated society or the educated person among the ignorant. If you enjoy Lawrence's stories and read further, you will find this a recurring theme in his novels and even in his own life.

You should find no difficulty comparing the approaches of Hardy and Lawrence to regional fiction: there is so much material on characters, plot and style. Why not look also at the opening description of Brinsley in 'Odour of Chrysanthemums' and compare it with one of Hardy's opening descriptions, for example in 'Fellow-Townsmen' or 'Interlopers at the Knap'?

Note: The 20th-century text you use in comparison need not be a short story (or stories) or even a work of prose fiction. In using D.H. Lawrence as a comparison, you could refer to his novels (e.g. *Sons and Lovers*) or a play like *The Widowing of Mrs Holroyd*.

Irony and misunderstanding

Many short stories depend for their effect on an ironic twist. Compare Hardy's use of this method with that of such 20th-century writers as "Saki" and Roald Dahl.

Irony, of course, depends on opposites, so misunderstanding (believing events to be the opposite of what they are) can be an effective form of irony. It is particularly effective in the short story, where the length and simplicity of plot make it comparatively easy for the central character or the reader to be "taken in". Hence the story can have a satisfying or shocking twist.

The best example in *Wessex Tales* is 'The Three Strangers'. Like many such stories, this operates in an enclosed setting (the shepherd's cottage) which enables Hardy to control the information his characters receive. You will often find this to be true in the other examples referred to later. The reader is deceived, but the main irony is directed at the powers of law-enforcement. This is a good-humoured use of ironic deception. Other Hardy stories suffer much more painful twists: the one that is most dependent on irony and misunderstanding is 'The Melancholy Hussar'.

Rather than concentrate on one author for the comparison, we are going to look at two authors whose short stories are in many schools' stock cupboards or libraries. "Saki" (H.H. Munro) wrote his short stories just before the First World War and 'The Lumber Room' is in many anthologies. Look in this case for the deliberate deception and the cruelty of the humour. The so-called aunt is led into a humiliating defeat by her determination to enforce her will. She is "thrown" by her own force and we rejoice in her downfall. Contrast Saki's lack of humanity with Hardy's broad human sympathy. Roald Dahl, in his more adult tales, is in some ways a Saki for the late 20th-century. 'The Landlady' is a tale of a similar persuasion – wickedly funny, with the reader seeing the truth before Billy Weaver. He is a much more sympathetic character than the aunt: does this make the twist more or less cruel?

There are many short stories that rely on this technique: you may choose quite different examples. You will probably remember Bill Naughton's stories for younger readers in *The Goalkeeper's Revenge*, in which many of the stories involve young people outwitting their "superiors". A more adult and much darker Naughton story with a double ironic twist is 'Late Night on Watling Street'. Whatever stories you choose, you should look at such factors as:

● Who is deceived into misunderstanding – the reader or the characters in the story?

● Is it deliberate deception or accidental misunderstanding?

● Where is the reader's sympathy (if there is any – some of the crueller stories remove all sympathy)?

- Is the story meant to convince within a real social setting? Hardy's tales have this aim: what about the others?
- Is the effect humorous, satisfying, pathetic, malicious, good-tempered…?

■ How to write an examination essay

Most of you will use *Wessex Tales* as Wide Reading coursework, but at least one examination board sets Hardy's stories as an examination text. Let us examine a sample essay title:

What makes 'The Melancholy Hussar of the German Legion' such a sad and unhappy tale? To what extent do the attitudes people had about relationships between men and women at this time affect the atmosphere of despair?

Answer the question asked

This is not asking you to re-tell the story (no credit is given for that), but to examine the mood of the tale. It also asks you to do three things, so you must do each of them at reasonable length. You must write about any relevant causes for the sadness of the story; you must show knowledge of attitudes to relationships between the sexes in the 19th century; and you must apply that knowledge to the overall atmosphere of the story.

Note: You are *not* told to give *only* those reasons for sadness which are related to attitudes to men-women relationships.

Approaching the question

Make notes of all the key points which you wish to bring into your essay. Many of these have been covered in the *Men and Women* and *Love* coursework sections, but here is a summary of some main points:

- the goodness of the two main characters, notably Matthaus;
- the misfortunes of chance, coincidence and misunderstandings;
- the vulnerability of women and the need for respectability;
- the use of the narrator to distance the events in time/Phyllis's later life;
- the bullying of the main characters, by a parent or by the system;
- the reasons for the characters acting as they did;
- the use of isolation and dependence;
- the emphasis on conventional behaviour.

Planning and ordering

Make a note by each main point to clarify at which stage in the essay you intend to use it to create a developing argument. You might, for instance, mark each point 1, 2 or 3 according to which of the three main tasks it relates to.

You will probably want to give each of the points either a single paragraph or several paragraphs, depending on its importance. You may wish to merge two of the points; you will certainly wish to place connected ideas next to each other.

Starting to write

You should attempt in the first paragraph to summarise the content of your response. The opening sentence should not be vague, but should direct the reader towards that response, for example: "In 'The Melancholy Hussar of the German Legion', Hardy presents us with a situation which is sad in itself (the death of two young men and Phyllis' life-long sense of loss) and develops it through the personalities of his characters and the social pressures they face." On the other hand, sentences such as "'The Melancholy Hussar' is about Phyllis Grove and Matthaus Tina and how he was executed as a deserter" are definitely not a good way to start.

During the essay

From time to time check your original list and make sure you cover all the points. Don't indulge yourself by writing at vast length on your favourite parts of the essay (or on your favourite title in the examination). Marks are gained most quickly at the start of an essay rather than after you have already made some good points. If time runs out, write brief notes to summarise the part you have no time for.

Don't worry about the final length. Some people write naturally at greater length than others and they don't always get the best marks. Use the time allowed valuably.

Use quotations when necessary, not because you like them. Quotations are most valuable when the way in which something is expressed matters; in other cases, a reference to the story can be just as useful. Even in an "open-book" examination, you must make sure that you do not have to search for quotations – there is too little time. By all means look up a quotation and check its exact words, but you need to know where to look.

■ Self-test answers

'The Three Strangers', 'A Tradition of Eighteen Hundred and Four', 'The Melancholy Hussar of the German Legion', 'The Withered Arm'

Who? What? Why? When? Where? How?
1 Conjurer Trendle (Arm)
2 The family mead-mug (Strangers)
3 The christening of their second daughter (Strangers)
4 30 June 1801 (Hussar)
5 Higher Crowstairs (Strangers)
6 By Trendle preparing egg and water to form a mirror (Arm)
7 Uncle Job (1804)
8 A white bonnet and a silver gown that whistled when it touched the pews (Arm)
9 Conscience and preserving her self-respect (Hussar)
10 1793 (Arm)
11 Lulworth Cove, by Selby's house (1804)
12 In song (Strangers)

Who said... about whom?
1 A milking woman about Gertrude Lodge (Arm)
2 Timothy Summers's brother about Timothy (Strangers)
3 Uncle Job about Napoleon (1804)
4 Farmer Lodge about his own son (Arm)
5 Humphrey Gould about Phyllis, referring to his present, a mirror (Hussar)
6 Matthaus about Christoph (Hussar)

Open quotations
1 "Her hair is lightish, and her face as comely as a live doll's" (Arm, Chap. 2)
2 "What woman would not pleased with such a handsome peace-offering?" (Hussar, Chap. 4)
3 "Here stretch the Downs, high and breezy and green, absolutely unchanged since those eventful days." (Hussar, opening sentence)
4 "The smile was neither mirthful nor sad, not precisely humorous nor altogether thoughtful." (Selby's "narrative smile", 1804, second paragraph)
5 "...so as when I raise en up and hit my prisoner 'tis made a lawful blow thereby." (Strangers, the constable and his staff)

Key sentences
1 Rhoda sees Gertrude touching the dead man (Arm, Chap. 9)
2 The third stranger sees his brother and the hangman (Strangers)
3 Napoleon's face is revealed (1804)
4 The execution of the hussars (Hussars, Chap. 5)
5 Rhoda throws off the incubus (Arm, Chap. 3)

Note the use of violent physical reaction (including shrieks and cries) by the characters in the story to emphasise to the reader how dramatic the events are.

Prove it!

1 Probably the best examples are Dr Grove, a retired physician; Lodge, a prosperous farmer, and his wife; and Humphrey Gould, the fashionable gentleman.

2 You can't prove anything definite, but you can show his sympathy for all the condemned men, either because of their characters (notably Matthaus) or because their crimes were understandable and not proven (Rhoda's son was just there at the wrong time). But the executioners are not cruel or terrifying.

3 Fennel lives in a remote place for his work, but enjoys company; Dr. Grove is simply unsociable; Trendle's conjuring puts him outside conventional society; Rhoda disappears for some time through grief and shame.

'Fellow-Townsmen', 'Interlopers at the Knap', 'The Distracted Preacher'

Who? What? Why? When? Where? How?

1 Lizzy Simpkins (later Newberry) (Preacher)
2 Architect (Townsmen)
3 "He had the prior claim." (Interlopers)
4 In September, four months after the near-drowning (Townsmen)
5 In the church tower and under a tree in the orchard (Preacher)
6 As a woman with long curls (Preacher)
7 Barnet (Townsmen)
8 The dress Darton sends to Sally (Interlopers)
9 To borrow mustard for a plaster for her father (Preacher)
10 On Sunday evening; church in the morning (Preacher)
11 At Chalk Newton, halfway between King's Hintock and Casterbridge (Interlopers)
12 300; nearly 260; 440 (Preacher)

Who said... about whom?

1 Barnet about Downe (Townsmen)
2 Japheth Johns about Sally; the actual quotation "I shouldn't call Sally Hall simple." (Interlopers)
3 Lizzy about Stockdale (Preacher)
4 Lizzy about Latimer (Preacher)
5 Downe about his first wife (Townsmen)
6 Lizzy about Stockdale (and herself) (Preacher)

Open quotations

1 "She no longer belongs to another... My poor brother is dead!" (Interlopers, Chap. 3)
2 "...he did not want the chicken, unless she brought it up herself." (Preacher, Chap. 1)
3 "She did wait – years and years –, but Barnet never reappeared." (Townsmen, last sentence)
4 "I want something more striking – more like a tomb I have seen in St. Paul's Cathedral." (Townsmen, Chap. 6)
5 "Nine of 'em are of your own congregation." (Preacher, Chap. 5)

Key sentences

1 Barnet deciding whether to attempt to revive his wife (Townsmen, Chap. 5)
2 Barnet on the news of her death (Townsmen, Chap. 8)
3 The "final" parting of Lizzy and Stockdale (Preacher, Chap. 7)
4 Sally Hall's last rejection of Darton (Interlopers, Chap. 5)
5 Stockdale's first clue that Lizzy is dressing as a man to go smuggling (Preacher, Chap. 3)

They emphasise that all these are love stories (and, indeed, stories about whom to marry). Despite Hardy's use of chance and coincidence, they also emphasise that the stories are about choice – each leads from or to a major decision by one or more characters.

Prove it!

1 You should have found plenty of evidence to support this view: failure to understand women; failure to understand their own feelings; bad timing. Stockdale is something of an exception, not so much because of the happy ending as because he has no doubt of his feelings and his dilemma (love v. career and belief) is possibly insoluble.
2 There are simple rustic characters: Ezra in 'Interlopers', for example. You should have found examples, though, of good judgement (Johns), cunning and ingenuity (the smugglers), plus simplicity among the educated (Stockdale).
3 'Townsmen': much the most urban – note how much depends on business, social position and class. Even the key building is a "chateau". 'Interlopers': remote village and the story is of people cut off from each other, interrupted and disastrous journeys, etc. 'Preacher': the most obvious, the smuggling community with its own traditions, a tale of smuggling and of conflicting moralities.